DAVID BECKHAM

Soccer's Superstar

Other titles in the **People to Know Today** series:

DAVID BECKHAM

Soccer's Superstar

By Tom Robinson

E

Enslow Publishers, Inc.
40 Industrial Road
Box 398
Berkeley Heights, NJ 07922
USA
http://www.enslow.com

Thank you to Dave Lauriha and my daughter, Bridgette, for sharing your love of soccer with me; and to my wife, Daria, and my daughters, Kasey and Bridgette, for their support.

Copyright © 2008 by Enslow Publishers, Inc.

Library of Congress Cataloging-in-Publication Data
Robinson, Tom.
  David Beckham : soccer's superstar / Tom Robinson.
    p. cm. — (People to know today)
  Summary: "A biography of English soccer player David Beckham"—Provided by publisher.
  Includes bibliographical references and index.
  ISBN-13: 978-0-7660-3110-4
  ISBN-10: 0-7660-3110-1
  1. Beckham, David, 1975—Juvenile literature. 2. Soccer players—England—Biography—Juvenile literature. 3. Celebrities—England—Biography—Juvenile literature. I. Title.
  GV942.7.B432R63 2008
  796.334092—dc22
  [B]

                    2007020303

Printed in the United States of America

10 9 8 7 6 5 4 3 2 1

To Our Readers: We have done our best to make sure all Internet addresses in this book were active and appropriate when we went to press. However, the author and publisher have no control over and assume no liability for the material available on those Internet sites or on other Web sites they may link to. Any comments or suggestions can be sent by e-mail to comments@enslow.com or to the address on the back cover.

Photos and Illustration: AP/Wide World, pp. 5, 6, 9, 13, 15, 16, 20, 26, 28, 31, 32, 36, 37, 45, 46, 51, 52, 54, 56, 58, 61, 63, 65, 67, 74, 77, 79, 86, 93.

Cover Illustration: AP/Wide World

CONTENTS

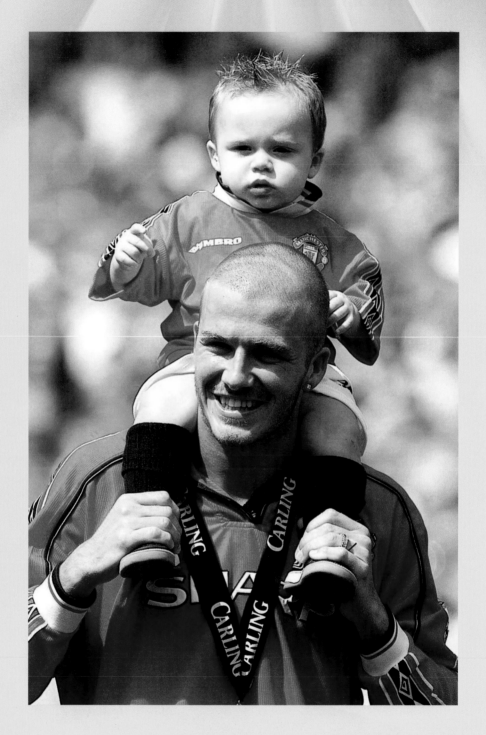

Manchester United's David Beckham carries his son, Brooklyn, on his shoulders after winning the English Premiership League soccer championship at Old Trafford, Manchester, England, on May 6, 2000.

1
COMING TO AMERICA

The *New York Times* faced a deadline and needed an answer. The newspaper's advertising department was holding space for a full-page color announcement. Situated on the East Coast, the *New York Times* was the first of several newspapers that needed to know whether to hold the space for the still unseen ad.

The marketing staff for Anschutz Entertainment Group (AEG) needed an answer from president and CEO Tim Leiweke by 6:00 A.M. Pacific time. Without an answer by then, the cost of canceling the ad and not even using the space would be $100,000 to AEG.

"I've got marketing guys yelling at me, going 'What do you want me to do? Are we going to run the ad or not?'" Leiweke said. "Pull the ad," he answered.[1]

The Best Ever

Pelé came out of retirement in 1975 to try to boost the North American Soccer League (NASL) and one of its high-profile franchises.

The NASL eventually folded after the 1984 season, but the Brazilian soccer star made the New York Cosmos a temporary success story. Behind Pelé and other imported stars, the Cosmos were the first soccer team to capture the nation's attention.

Pelé was the highest scorer in Brazilian soccer history and the only player to be on three World Cup championship teams. He was thirty-five when he came to the United States, but the striker's dazzling ball-handling and scoring skills helped him win the NASL Most Valuable Player Award in 1976.

The International Olympic Committee named Pelé the Athlete of the Century.

With so much money at stake, the *New York Times* responded by giving AEG a twenty-minute extension to decide for sure. The history of American professional soccer—and the look of the full-color page in the next day's *New York Times*—changed dramatically in those twenty minutes.

During that time, Leiweke learned that AEG, which owned Major League Soccer's Los Angeles Galaxy, had information to share with the entire country. David Beckham's representatives called at 6:10 A.M. to confirm that the man who was arguably the sport's biggest international star was ready to sign a contract to continue his career in the United States. The AEG staff spent the rest of Thursday, January 10 arranging those full-page newspaper ads that would appear on January 11, the same day the team would hold a teleconference introducing Beckham as the newest and brightest star on the Galaxy.

Beckham had long been the subject of speculation about a possible move to the United States and Major League Soccer (MLS). That speculation had just become reality. With fame extending beyond the playing field and a pop music star for a wife, there was only one fitting place for the Beckham family to settle. Hollywood was the place. The Los Angeles Galaxy announced the signing of Beckham, signaling a renewed effort to bring attention to the sport across the United States.

The desired reaction was immediate. The news of Beckham's announcement was discussed in many media outlets, including those that often do not commit time or space to soccer. The MLS had never received as much attention at any other time in its twelve-year

Pelé (right, No. 10) came out of retirement to give a boost to the North American Soccer League in the 1970s. Pele played for the New York Cosmos for three years before stepping away in front of a sellout crowd at Giants Stadium in New Jersey.

history. The Galaxy sold 5,000 season tickets in less than forty-eight hours, Leiweke told *Sports Illustrated.*

The process that ultimately brought Beckham to Los Angeles, however, was long and involved. *Sports Illustrated* traced the first steps to five years earlier. Leiweke met Terry Byrne, one of Beckham's managers, in London in 2002 to discuss the possibility of putting a branch of Beckham's new soccer academy at the Home Depot Center, which was being built as the new home stadium for the Galaxy.

Beckham shot a commercial at the Home Depot Center in 2003. Leiweke was often in contact with Simon Fuller, a music promoter who managed some of the business interests of Beckham and his wife, Victoria, formerly known as Posh Spice from the Spice Girls. Following a 2005 exhibition game in which Beckham's Real Madrid team pounded an MLS All-Star team, 5–0, Leiweke and Beckham had a dinner meeting in Spain along with MLS officials, including commissioner Don Garber.

"Tim had already done the academy deal, and we filled David in on our league," Garber said.[2]

There was clearly interest on both sides but nothing close to a commitment. Beckham was under contract until 2007 with Real Madrid, and the MLS had rules in place to limit salaries. With revenue nowhere close to matching the four major sports leagues in the United States, the MLS was trying to be careful not to commit to too many costs that could put the future of the league in jeopardy. A previous U.S. professional league, the North American Soccer League, had gone out of business.

Beckham's fame simply made him worth too much money to settle on a contract that fit within Major League Soccer's tight salary cap.

After the signing was announced, a new subject took over speculation surrounding Beckham. At thirty-one years old when he signed, how much could Beckham change the MLS during the next five years?

The league had already changed for Beckham. Leiweke proposed a rule change at the MLS Board of Governors in 2005, but it was shot down. In November 2006, the rule change passed. The new rule allowed each team to have one designated player making an unlimited salary as long as the individual owner committed to paying everything above $400,000 a year. Unofficially, the rule became known as "The Beckham Rule" long before it was used to bring him to the United States.

> **Beckham's fame made him worth too much money to settle on a contract that fit within Major League Soccer's tight salary cap.**

Leiweke confirmed the commitment of team owner Phil Anschutz. Then Leiweke started working on contract proposals that he could discuss with Beckham when his contract with Real Madrid allowed him to negotiate elsewhere at the start of 2007.

Although his status on the team had slipped somewhat, Beckham reportedly was still offered a new two-year contract with Real Madrid. Other European teams were interested as well. Beckham's power, which created bending free kicks and effective crossing passes from his midfield position, made him a sought-after player. The Galaxy needed to produce an impressive offer.

The contract Beckham eventually signed was immediately referred to as being worth $250 million. That could prove to be true, but his soccer contract with the Galaxy was actually worth $50 million—$10 million a year for five years—plus provisions for him to make much more off jersey sales and shares of other revenue increases the team shows after his signing.

"There are certain aspects of the deal that are ultimately about the upside value of the league as a whole that David can participate in," Leiweke said. "Our partners all had to sign off, and they did. We had a couple of interesting board calls, but they did."[3]

The deal was in place, and Beckham was the first player to be signed under "The Beckham Rule."

"I'm coming there to be a part of a team, to work hard and hopefully win things," Beckham said during

the teleconference to announce his contract. "With me, it's about football [soccer]. I'm coming there to make a difference. I'm coming there to play football."[4]

The Galaxy certainly hoped for help on the field from Beckham, but from the moment the contract was signed there was no question that more was expected from him.

Beckham (right) speaks with Tim Leiweke of the Anschutz Entertainment Group during a press conference where a partnership to establish The David Beckham Academy was announced in 2005.

"I'm not saying me coming over to the States is going to make soccer the biggest sport in America," Beckham said. "That would be difficult to achieve. Baseball, basketball, American football, they've been around. But I wouldn't be doing this if I didn't think I could make a difference."[5]

Those who have invested the league's reputation in Beckham clearly expect such an impact.

"David Beckham is a global sports icon who will transcend the sport of soccer in America," Garber, the MLS commissioner, said. "His decision to continue his storied career in Major League Soccer is a testament to the fact that America is rapidly becoming a true 'Soccer Nation' with Major League Soccer at the core."[6]

> **"David Beckham is a global sports icon who will transcend the sport of soccer in America."**

Leiweke convinced his colleagues around the league to see what Beckham could do for the MLS.

"David Beckham will have a greater impact on soccer in America than any athlete has ever had on a sport globally," Leiweke said. "We are acquiring an individual that will not only be the best ambassador and the best role model for athletes and fans of soccer but the best example of what an athlete can and should be. David is truly the only individual that can build a 'bridge' between soccer in America and the rest of the world."[7]

During Beckham's time at home in England early in his professional career, his Manchester United team was the richest soccer club in the world. When Beckham jumped to Real Madrid in 2003, the sales of jerseys and other merchandise increased so much that his new team replaced Manchester United as the biggest money-producing club in the sport.

"I have played for two of the biggest clubs in football, and I

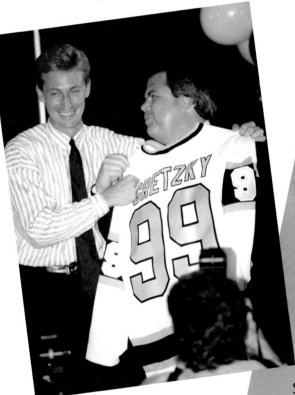

Wayne Gretzky (left) was all smiles after being traded in 1988 to the Los Angeles Kings, owned by Bruce McNall (right).

The Great One

David Beckham was not the first athlete brought in to try to boost the status of a sport in the United States through exposure in Los Angeles.

The Los Angeles Kings of the National Hockey League traded for Wayne Gretzky, the most prolific scorer in the sport's history, on August 9, 1988. Gretzky was at the peak of his career, having led the Edmonton Oilers to four Stanley Cups as NHL champion.

There were other similarities to the Beckham situation. Gretzky's new wife, actress Janet Jones, fit in Los Angeles.

There were also differences. Soccer has already taken hold in the United States on the youth participation level but has not arrived as a spectator sport. Gretzky's task was to help build hockey in California on all levels.

Beckham (center) holds up his new jersey as he is introduced as the newest member of the Los Angeles Galaxy soccer team during a news conference at the Home Depot Center.

look forward to the new challenge of growing the world's most popular game in a country that is as passionate about its sports as my own," Beckham said.[8]

Leiweke and his staff have big plans for using Beckham's fame to vastly increase the sales of Los Angeles Galaxy products.

"We made a decision that it was time to start thinking through how we create a more worldly brand," Leiweke said. "We have a good name. Galaxy works. But we need a more legendary, traditional kind of look that's more of a soccer look."[9]

The team plans to change its look, getting rid of its green-and-gold jerseys.

"When I think of the Galaxy, I think of dark blue," Galaxy general manager Alexi Lalas said.[10]

Leiweke pictures fans wearing Galaxy jerseys with Beckham's name and number twenty-three. His vision of Beckham's impact was already proving accurate in the first days after the signing was announced.

Not all of the newspaper space devoted to Beckham's future with the team was in the form of paid advertisements.

"We went through two years of arguments within Major League Soccer: Is the designated player a good idea or a bad idea? Two years. We went through everything with David on his vision and the academy, telling him, 'If you ever make a decision that you want to come, it's going to work. Here's why, and let us know,'" Leiweke said. "We went through all the rumors of other clubs' interest, went through the hell of the ten days negotiating the contract, and when you sat there today and opened up the paper … [you] saw five pages of articles in the Los Angeles Times."[11]

Before he ever kicked a ball in a professional soccer game in the United States, Beckham was already increasing the sport's exposure around the country.

2

STARTING EARLY

Ted Beckham never quite reached his dream of a career as a soccer professional. He did, however, stay active as a player in local leagues and was ready to help coach youngsters, including his son, David.

David Beckham was born May 2, 1975, in Leytonstone, England. He was the second of Ted and Sandra Beckham's three children.

Leytonstone is a blue-collar town north of London and, like much of England, is a soccer hotbed.

David went to watch his father's games and always seemed to have his own soccer ball to work on his foot-work and ball-handling skills. One of the activities of David's Boy Scout troop was playing soccer. David showed natural ability playing other sports, such as rounders, baseball, basketball, and rugby, but it was soccer that drew most of his interest.

Birthday and Christmas gifts were easy to determine in the Beckham house. Whether it was a ball, a jersey, or a poster of a famous player, any soccer gift was a wise choice for David.

It did not take David long to show he had special talents to go with his interest in the game. As an eight-year-old, he scored more than one hundred goals for the Ridgeway Rovers of the Enfield District League. David seemed to be able to read plays before they happened and had the ability to make the most of all the opportunities that anticipation gave him.

David's father had worked with him on passing and dribbling. The youngster was impressive at both, but what he developed the most was his shooting ability. David had a powerful right leg, capable of producing hard shots that traveled far and fast. He also began

Rounders, Baseball Are Similar

Rounders is an English sport, played mostly by boys, that has many similarities to and may have been a predecessor to baseball.

Rounders has four posts and one open side in a five-sided shape similar to the four-sided diamond and bases in baseball.

A batter stands at the batting square, 8.5 meters (28 feet) from the bowling square. A bowler, similar to a baseball pitcher, throws the ball over the batting square, above the knee and below the head of the batter. The batter tries to hit the ball and proceed around to four posts.

A runner is out if the ball is caught on the fly or a fielder touches him while running between posts. Unlike baseball, there is no foul territory.

developing the gift of making the longer shots curl. This allowed him to fool goalies and start the long history of scoring goals that left observers shaking their heads.

David reached new levels during his appearances at the Bobby Charlton Soccer Schools as an eleven-, twelve-, and thirteen-year-old. David was tested on the Bobby Charlton Soccer Schools Skills Test and gained first place in his group, earning a spot in the National Skills Final at Old Trafford, the home of Manchester United, his favorite team. By winning the skills contest, David's prize was to get to spend one week with the FC Barcelona in Spain.

Bobby Charlton called David the best eleven-year-old he had seen. At the time, it was Charlton's sixth year running the school,

Manchester United's legend Bobby Charlton called Beckham the best eleven-year-old he had ever seen.

which is still active. David's performances there for three summers were memorable for current coaching director Bryn Cooper, who directed one of the courses at the time.

"David had tremendous ability as a young boy," Cooper said. "Such was his ability that in 1988 he was transferred from the thirteen-year-old age group to an older age group. Despite this, David still achieved the highest skills score in this older group."[1]

Cooper said it was clear that David wanted more from his soccer abilities.

"In addition to his natural ability, David displayed a fantastic work ethic and a great deal of determination, which meant he was continually practicing his individual skills," Cooper said. "It was clearly evident to the coaches at Bobby Charlton Soccer Schools that David was completely focused on becoming a professional footballer."[2]

Just as a star high school athlete in the United States would be recruited by colleges, David was sought after by club teams but at an even younger age.

David had first been seen by scouts of Manchester United while playing for his Waltham Forest Under-12 team. David was invited to training sessions and tryouts with Manchester United in addition to his chance to serve as a mascot for a game.

Whenever it was possible for him to be there, David was happy with Manchester United, the club he, along with his parents, grew up cheering for. Although he tried out with Leyton Orient and trained with the Tottenham Hotspur, both local clubs, the chance to be part of the Manchester United program was a dream come true.

David signed schoolboy forms, committing to Manchester United, which was based about 322 kilometers (200 miles) from home, on his fourteenth birthday. Advice from Bobby Charlton helped clinch the deal. David signed a Youth Training Scheme contract with the club July 8, 1991, when he was sixteen. David was part of a powerful youth team, joining Ryan Giggs, Gary Neville, and Paul Scholes to help Manchester United win the FA Youth Cup in 1992. He scored a goal in the final against Crystal Palace.

David signed a contract with the club when he was sixteen.

By this time, David was already beginning his transition to Manchester United's top team. He did, however, helped Manchester United to a runner-up finish in the 1993 FA Youth Cup and to the reserve team league championship in 1994. The United reserve team allowed young players like Beckham to gain experience.

3

PROFESSIONAL PROMOTION

The message can be a difficult one for a young player to receive. A position on a team at the highest level of sports has been attained but then taken away. A move to a lower level is needed to get a chance to play more and continue the development of a promising career.

As a nineteen-year-old, David Beckham received just such a message from Manchester United team manager Alex Ferguson. By 1994, David had spent significant time with the Manchester United first team, but he was not playing much. David had found success in the Manchester United program with the junior team in the Youth Cup and with the reserve team.

Football Association Structure

David Beckham's Manchester United teams routinely competed for the two most sought-after titles in English soccer.

The Football Association (FA) was organized in 1863 to unify soccer rules throughout England. The FA ran a championship, called the Challenge Cup, beginning in 1871. The FA has since evolved into several layers of league competition.

The Premier League, also known as the Premiership, is the highest-level professional league within the FA. The Premier League champion also earns a chance to play in the Champions League with winners from throughout Europe.

Following league competition, the Football Association Challenge Cup, known in short as the "FA Cup," is contested. The FA Cup was held at Wembley Stadium in London in 1923.

To give David more experience as a first-team player, Ferguson was sending him to Preston North End, a lower-level professional team. Proving he was good enough to play in the Premier League also meant proving he was too good to be contained on a third-level professional team.

David quickly made an impression with Preston North End. He curled a corner kick into the net for a goal in his first game. He played four more games, scoring another goal. David's strong play and the need for help when a shortage of available players developed on the Manchester United active roster meant the end of his time with Preston North End after just five games.

Coach Gary Peters surprised some of Preston North End's veteran players when he put David ahead of the players who regularly took free kicks and corner kicks. David managed, however, to win over his skeptical teammates.

"In the end, we had to admit that he was quite good," Preston North End teammate Ryan Kidd said. "He was here just over a month and he was absolutely fantastic."[1]

David was a leader of the championship Youth team in 1992, but by the end of the year, he was already climbing the professional soccer ladder within the Manchester United program. He was promoted to the first team roster in October. He entered a game for the first time as a substitute for Andrei Kanchelskis in the second round of the League Cup against Brighton and Hove Albion.

David hoped the chance to substitute late in 1992 was a sign that he would soon be a first-team player on a regular basis. David moved up to practicing with the first team in January 1993, but playing time was slow to come. His first full game was not until September 1994 against Port Vale in a League Cup game. The first goal came in November 1994 against Galatasaray, a Turkish team, in the Champions League.

Progress came soon after the return from Preston North End.

Several key players finished their careers with Manchester United, leaving Ferguson with a decision to make prior to the 1995–96 season. Paul Ince left to play in Italy for Inter Milan; Mark Hughes was sold to Chelsea; and Kanchelskis was sold to Everton. Ferguson decided to turn to his promising youngsters,

Beckham (right) and England teammate Nicky Butt prepare for a 2003 training session in Vaduz, Liechtenstein.

including David, rather than spend money on high-priced, established talent. Not all of the Manchester United fans were convinced Ferguson was making the right move.

In the season opener, Aston Villa defeated Manchester United, 3–1, despite David's first Premier League goal. The questions increased. Television commentator Alan Hansen of the British Broadcasting Company (BBC) was among the skeptics.

"You can't win anything with kids," Hansen said.[2]

However, the youngsters, known as "Fergie's Fledglings," proved Ferguson correct and Hansen and others wrong. Brothers Gary and Phil Neville, Paul Scholes, and Nicky Butt joined David in leading the team to wins in its next five games.

Following a slip to the middle of the pack, Manchester United made a steady rise through the standings. A 3–0 win against

> The **youngsters,** known as **"Fergie's Fledglings,"** proved Hansen and others **wrong.**

Middlesbrough in the final game completed the climb to first place. David scored eight goals along the way, including several on free kicks.

The young lineup, which featured players with an average age of twenty-four, was no problem by the time the season ended and Cup play started. Manchester United edged Chelsea, 2–1, on March 31 to reach the May 1 championship game.

When Eric Cantona scored the game's only goal in the final for a 1–0 win against Liverpool, Manchester United completed the double of winning both the Premier League and the FA Cup.

Beckham (right) jokes with England teammate Gary Neville during a training session at Old Trafford, Manchester in 2005.

David's fame soared at the start of the 1996–97 season. Manchester United played Wimbledon at Selhurst Park in the Premier League season opener.

As David reached midfield with the ball, he noticed Wimbledon goalie Neil Sullivan a few steps too far out in front of the goal. David launched a looping kick, half the length of the field, over Sullivan's head for a goal. The goal was replayed over and over on television in England.

"I've never seen it done," Manchester United coach Alex Ferguson said. "Everyone is scratching their heads in the dressing room to try to remember something similar. Pelé in 1970 is the only one."[3]

Manchester United picked up steam later in the 1996–97 season, going on a late-season run of fifteen games without a loss. The last game in the streak was against Chelsea when David's late goal forced a tie. Manchester United won its second league title in a row and reached the semifinals of the Champions League before losing.

David launched a looping kick, half the length of the field, over Sullivan's head for a goal.

David was runner-up in voting for EA Player of the Year and won the voting for Young Player of the Year.

4
CELEBRITY LIFE

Full names are not really needed in Europe for David Beckham and his wife, Victoria. "Posh and Becks" is all the reference needed for most people to know the soccer star and his musician wife are again the topic of conversation.

Separately, David Beckham and Victoria Adams, also known as Posh Spice from the music group the Spice Girls, already attracted plenty of attention. When two of England's most famous young adults began dating in 1997, that only served to increase the individual fame that each had attained.

The Spice Girls managed nine number-one hits in England, the most ever by a female group. The only artists ever to have more number-one hits were The Beatles, Elvis Presley, Cliff Richard, and Madonna.

British pop group The Spice Girls (including Victoria Adams, far left) promote their movie *Spice World* in Chicago in 1998.

The group began forming in 1994, put its five members together in 1995, and released songs in 1996. From then until 1998, the Spice Girls were the hottest act in the music business. Proclaiming "Girl Power," the group appealed to teenage and younger girls. They even appeared together in the movie *Spice World*.

Geri Halliwell, known as Ginger Spice, left the group in 1998 to start a solo career and the momentum slowed. The Spice Girls were back, however, in 2000 with their ninth number-one hit, "Holler Holler/Let Love Lead the Way."

"We are so happy because we have put in a lot of hard work," Victoria said when the song became a hit

The exclusive Luttrellstown Castle mansion near Dublin was the venue for the wedding of Beckham and Spice Girl Victoria Adams.

late in 2000. "The fans have been brilliant, and we really appreciate how loyal they've been to us."[1]

Victoria (Posh Spice), Emma Bunton (Baby Spice), Melanie Chisholm (Sporty Spice), and Melanie Brown (Scary Spice) were still with the group at the time, but they parted ways soon after. Eventually each went on to her own solo career. Although Victoria never matched the number-one hits the others produced, she did have several songs that reached the top ten in England.

Posh and Becks were practically regarded as royalty in England. Their wedding was fittingly held at a castle. Security guards limited access to 200-plus, mostly famous, invited guests at Luttrellstown Castle in Ireland for the July 4, 1999, wedding. A single dove was released as a symbol of their love as David and Victoria were pronounced man and wife.

Manchester United teammate Gary Neville was David's best man. Members of the Spice Girls and the Manchester United and English national soccer teams were among the guests.

David and Victoria sat on golden thrones at the lavish dinner. An orchestra and fireworks display were part of the reception.

Commercial endorsements and a famous wife only served to increase the exposure Beckham received as a stylish soccer star. His income from endorsements was often more than double what he received for playing soccer.

"David Beckham is a sports marketer's dream—talented, photo-genic and with a pop-star wife," said Alex Chapman, a partner at Briffa, a London law firm specializing in intellectual property and entertainment law. "He is the England captain, arguably England's most gifted player and almost certainly the world's most famous footballer."[2]

When Beckham moved from Manchester United to Real Madrid, sales of shirts with his name and

> **David and Victoria sat on golden thrones at the lavish dinner.**

number twenty-three reached record highs. Manchester United had been the most profitable soccer club in the world, but that title transferred with Beckham to Real Madrid.

"He is almost **certainly** the world's **most famous footballer.**"

"Beckham's commercial potential is seen by many to outweigh his gifts on the pitch. It was particularly noteworthy that Real Madrid opted to pursue the services of Mr. Beckham ahead of those of Brazilian international and World Cup winner Ronaldinho because of Beckham's perceived superior marketability. As such, David Beckham typifies the importance of commercial factors in modern sport," Chapman said.[3]

Soccer fans can—and do—debate whether Beckham is the best player in the world. What is hard to debate is that he is the most famous. In 2003 and 2004, "David Beckham" was the most queried sports personality on the Internet search engine google.com.

Fame makes Beckham an obvious choice for companies seeking a celebrity endorsement. Adidas, Disney, Gillette, Pepsi, Snickers, and cell phone company Vodafone are among those that have used him prominently. Many more have asked.

"I get many offers for commercial associations, but I only ever consider the ones that I feel are right," Beckham said.[4]

Companies understand the value of being associated with Beckham's name. Audi-Volkswagen international, the automobile sponsor of Real Madrid, made sure not to miss an opportunity when Beckham's signing with the team became imminent in 2003. Arrangements were made to make sure Audis were provided for Beckham when he arrived in the city. Audi officials were thrilled when Beckham was filmed and photographed getting in and out of their cars as he went to several meetings.

"If Audi had tried to carry off an equivalent ad campaign—one in which we received so much exposure on prime-time TV and on front pages of newspapers in virtually every country in the world—it would have been, quite simply, unpayable," Audi Spain president Jesus Gasanz said. "In order to pay for that quality of advertising we would have had to sell the company first. I repeat, what we got during those 36 hours was unpayable."[5]

Being famous is not always a favorable situation. Fame can make people like David and Victoria targets of more than autograph seekers.

There have been media reports of alleged sabotage of Beckham's Ferrari, attempts to break in to their home, and plots to kidnap their son Brooklyn.

The interest in their lives seemed distorted at times. Beckham, while out of the lineup with an injury, visited with the queen of England, sparking a

Charitable Contributions

David Beckham has been involved in many charitable projects, including UNICEF, which he has supported from the time he was playing with Manchester United.

UNICEF, the United Nation's Children's Fund, named Beckham as a goodwill ambassador for its Sports for Development program on January 12, 2005. Beckham's first official function after being named goodwill ambassador was to visit workers who were preparing items to send to Indian Ocean tsunami victims and to film a public service announcement appealing for more donations.

"People have been so generous to date and it is important that they continue to donate money to organizations such as UNICEF to help in aid relief and reconstruction," Beckham said.

controversy among those who thought he should be with his team. When their son Romeo fell in public as a toddler and needed two stitches, the incident became front-page news in many English newspapers.

Manchester United pledged to assist UNICEF in Beijing.

"I just see myself as a footballer more than anything, and the other side is a bonus," Beckham said. "That's the way I actually look at it. The stuff that goes on around me is a bonus, and the reason it's a bonus is because I'm a footballer, and that's the way I treat it."[6]

Beckham sits with his sons Brooklyn (left) and Romeo (right) as they watch a tennis match in Madrid, Spain, in 2004.

5
TRIPLE CROWN

The level of competition, the balance between the teams, and the conservative, low-scoring nature of professional soccer all conspire to make dominating difficult. Seldom does the same team emerge as the best in England's Premier League throughout the season and then again in the shorter tournament-style FA Cup play that follows.

In the first 105 years of organized English soccer, only five teams had won both titles. Two of those came in the first eleven years. The Tottenham Hotspur achieved the double in 1961, Arsenal did it in 1971, and Liverpool won both in 1986.

Manchester United started changing that in 1994. When the 1998–99 season began, it already had two doubles to its credit.

Coming off a 1997–98 season in which it had surprisingly failed to win any titles, Manchester United embarked on a series of dramatic results that led to an amazing achievement. Manchester United won The Treble—or triple—when it took the FA Premier League, FA Cup, and Champions League titles.

"English football has been in the wilderness for a long time, and now we're back on the world stage," former English soccer star Bobby Charlton said. "It's been all right saying English football is the healthiest and the best to watch, but you really need to have something to show for it, and to win the Champions League, there's nothing bigger in world club football."[1]

David Beckham opened the 1998–99 season as the object of strong criticism for the ejection he had received in the 1998 World Cup. He was jeered throughout the league but gradually regained the support of Manchester United fans with a strong season.

After ten months of play, Manchester United and Arsenal were still jostling for position at the top of the Premier League standings. In the final game of the season, Manchester United knew the only way to be sure of its fifth Premier League championship in seven years was to come away with a win against the Tottenham Hotspur.

Rio Ferdinand got behind the Manchester United defense and lofted a shot over goalkeeper Peter Schmeichel in the twenty-fourth minute. Manchester

United was forced to play from behind. As the first half neared its conclusion, Manchester United put together chance after chance, including a header that Beckham sent over the crossbar. Beckham made up for it with less than six minutes remaining in the half when he took a cross from Ryan Giggs and blasted a shot from the right side of the penalty area for a 1–1 tie.

Andy Cole entered the game at the start of the second half. He needed less than two minutes to take a pass from Gary Neville and convert it into the winning goal in a 2–1 victory.

Teams are awarded three points in the standings for each win and one for each tie. Manchester United finished the season with one more point in the standings than Arsenal.

The end of league play and the start of Cup competition overlap in England. So, by the time Manchester United rallied past the Tottenham Hotspur to finish first in the Premier League, it had already made it through a grueling Cup semifinal with Arsenal.

> **Teams** are awarded **three** points in the standings for **each** **win** and **one** for each **tie.**

Manchester United and Arsenal had already played to a tie, forcing a replay of the semifinal. The teams were still difficult to separate in the rematch.

Beckham gave Manchester United the early lead by tucking a 23-meter (25-yard) shot just inside the far post. Arsenal tied the game in the second half and appeared to be in position to produce the win two minutes into injury time. Ray Parlour broke into the penalty area and was tackled illegally by Phil Neville, setting up a penalty kick for the potential game-winner. Arsenal went with Dennis Bergkamp, who had already scored the tying goal, for the shot. Schmeichel came up with the stop, and the game moved into overtime.

Giggs took control of the ball on his own side of midfield nineteen minutes into overtime. Methodically, he controlled his dribble, moving past four defenders, weaving his way into close range for the game-winning shot.

With the Premier League title in its possession, Manchester United proceeded to the FA Cup Final on May 22, 1999, at Wembley Stadium against Newcastle United.

An injury to team captain Roy Keane early in the game brought Teddy Sheringham off the Manchester United bench. Sheringham took all of a minute and thirty-six seconds to score the game's first goal.

Beckham, who began his career as a center mid-fielder, had by this point been used more as a right midfielder because of his ability to cross the ball to his teammates. Injuries forced adjustments that put him back in the middle where more controlled passing is often the method needed to succeed. Beckham kept the Manchester United attack running efficiently and kept control of the game.

Paul Scholes had helped set up Sheringham's first-half goal. In the second half, the combination worked in the opposite way with Scholes putting in the goal that completed the scoring in the 2–0 victory.

The seasons all move toward the finish line together, with each championship being followed shortly thereafter by the pursuit of another more prestigious title. Manchester United was playing in the Champions League because of its status as one of the top two teams in England the season before.

Manchester United now had another double, but what made it a true cause for celebration was that the team was only one win from The Treble. Manchester United had already made the most impressive of its comebacks in the Champions League semifinal on the way to the final, which is also known as the European Cup.

Giggs had scored a goal in the final minute to get a 1–1 tie with Juventus to force a replay of the semifinal. In the replay, Manchester United again found itself behind, this time, 2–0, on a pair of goals by Filippo Inzaghi in the first eleven minutes.

This Manchester United team, however, was not an easy one to put away. Juventus, a powerful Italian team that had been to the previous three European Cup finals, could not hold Manchester United down.

One way for Manchester United to start a comeback was to take advantage of a corner kick by putting Beckham's best skills to work. Midway through the first half, Beckham floated a kick out in front of the goal. Keane went up above two defenders to snap a header into the net.

The game was not even close to reaching halftime yet when Manchester United forced a tie. Dwight Yorke dove through the air, leaving himself parallel to the ground, to get his head on the ball. He sent a shot into the net for the second Manchester United goal.

Keane drew a yellow card, his second of the tournament, when he tripped Zidane of Juventus. The yellow card was Keane's first of the game, but second of the tournament, meaning he would be ineligible for the European Cup final. All Keane

> **One** way for **Manchester United** to start a **comeback** was by putting Beckham's best **skills** to work.

could do was try to help his team get to the final and then watch from there.

With the teams still deadlocked, 2–2, Paul Scholes also picked up his second yellow card of the tournament and found himself with the same fate as Keane.

With about seven minutes remaining, Yorke broke into the Juventus end where he was tripped. The ball popped loose, and Andy Cole was there to pound it into the net for the winning goal.

No team from England had ever won The Treble of the Premier League, FA Cup, and European Cup. The absence of Keane and Scholes meant lineup juggling. Beckham was back in the playmaking role of center midfielder as Manchester United took on Bayern Munich from Germany on May 26, 1999, in the final in Barcelona.

The resulting contest was fitting for such a historic occasion for English soccer.

Bayern Munich came to the end of regulation time with a 1–0 lead. Three minutes of time was left to replace stoppage time during the match. The championship trophy was being prepared with Bayern Munich's colors being added to it.

Out on the field, Beckham noticed the trophy being brought to the Bayern Munich sideline.

"I saw the cup on its way down with Bayern's colors on it," he said. "Yet two minutes later, it was ours."[2]

As was the case throughout much of the run to The Treble, plays by Beckham and some key substitutes accounted for a change of fortunes.

Bayern Munich led from the fifth minute all the way into stoppage time. Sheringham entered the game in the sixty-seventh minute, shuffling the midfield. Ole

Gunnar Solskjaer came on in the eighty-first minute. Beckham was back at his right midfield position, trying desperately to help Manchester United generate more offense.

Beckham takes a free kick for Manchester United as the Bayern Munich players jump to defend their goal during their 1999 UEFA Champions Cup final match in Barcelona, Spain.

Beckham drove down the right side, setting up a Gary Neville cross, which went off the end line off a Bayern Munich player, to set up a corner kick. The defense almost got the ball out of the penalty area, but Giggs was there to send a shot toward the post. Sheringham got to the ball before it could go wide and redirected it into the net from just 5.5 meters (6 yards) away. Bayern Munich went from spending almost an entire game cautiously

A Little Help

Many Manchester United fans believed their team had a guiding spirit when it captured the Champions League title.

The European Cup final came on what would have been the ninetieth birthday of Matt Busby, who survived a 1958 plane crash to lead Manchester United to its only previous Champions League title in 1968.

protecting a one-goal lead to needing to find a way to break a tie. Overtime and a golden goal for the championship seemed likely, but Manchester United had the momentum.

Solskjaer applied the pressure that led to another corner kick. Beckham, of course, was called on to start the play that could lift his team into the history books. Sheringham went the highest in the crowd and flicked a header toward the front of the goal. With attention drawn to trying to play the

Manager Matt Busby (middle) guided Manchester United to the Champions League title in 1968. Beckham helped United to its second Champions Cup crown in 1999.

original corner kick, Solskjaer had broken loose. Solskjaer got to the ball first and quickly hooked a shot up into the top of the goal 2:17 into the three extra minutes.

The last shot of the season was the biggest. It showed the ability of a championship team to win against tremendous odds.

"The most important factor was the spirit of the team," Manchester United coach Alex Ferguson said. "They just never give in; they don't know how to. A manager can talk about tactics, but if the players can't bring that inner beast out of them then he's wasting his team. Well, they've got the beast inside them and found it when it mattered. People will never forget this team, my '94 double-winning side had a mental toughness about them, but this crop are the best. They have proved that . . . they are legends."[3]

The season created a lifetime of memories for Beckham.

"My best experience is winning The Treble for United, winning the European Cup," he said. "For me, the experience in '99, there's no bigger and better feeling than that."[4]

6
BEND IT LIKE BECKHAM

David Beckham's ability to curve a soccer ball on long arching kicks is a rare skill. After all, not many athletic traits inspire a movie, articles in technical journals, and discussions of how to use sports to teach students about physics.

Most important in learning how to "bend it like Beckham," a player needs to try to develop the skill to do it instinctively.

Beckham is not thinking about the laws of physics as he approaches the ball for a corner, direct, or indirect kick. A natural feeling, built through years of practice, takes over as instincts translate the thought of what he wants to do into the angle and speed with which he swings his leg.

"His judgment of distance and power is amazing," former Brazilian soccer star Zico Na Rede said.[1]

That feel has produced two World Cup goals off direct kicks and countless unstoppable shots. It has also contributed heavily to making Beckham the most famous soccer player of his era.

Beckham is an excellent passer, a strong goal scorer for a midfielder, and a tremendously conditioned and competitive athlete. All of those traits have combined to make him one of the best players in the world. The trademark free kicks, however, are what have made him the most famous.

The sporting goods company adidas even tried to duplicate the position of Beckham's body on free kicks when it designed the logo for its products that feature him.

"We wanted to capture the unique nature of a Beckham free kick," said Eric Vellozzi, who designed the logo for

What Makes a Beckham Kick Bend

Bending the ball when kicking it in soccer requires striking the ball off-center with the side of the foot. If a player kicks the ball with his or her foot aiming directly at the target and makes contact in the center of the ball, based on that path, it will travel straight.

Striking the ball from an angle, off-center, usually with the inside of the foot, can make the ball curve. The spin resulting from striking the ball this way is part of what makes it curve. For that curve to be noticeable, the ball has to be struck hard enough because the curve takes place as the ball loses speed while flying through the air.

The angle at which the foot is positioned relative to the leg also contributes to the height at which the ball travels and how it curves.

Movie Time

Bend It Like Beckham, the movie, was released in England in 2002 and the United States in 2003.

The movie was filmed and set in London. Keira Knightley and Parminder Nagra star as two young women from London who come from different backgrounds but share a love of soccer and an appreciation of David Beckham's skills.

The movie's soundtrack includes music from Victoria Beckham and another former Spice Girl, Melanie C.

David Beckham is shown in the movie in footage from his games. David and Victoria had originally planned to make a cameo appearance in the movie, but lookalikes wound up playing them because of a scheduling conflict.

adidas. "A David Beckham free kick is one of the most recognizable images in world sport, even before he kicks the ball, due to the angle of his body upon impact. Couple that with the significant curve that this action puts on the flight path of the ball and you have something truly original."[2]

Beckham likes the impact of the logo.

"The logo is totally me and something that people can relate to," he said. "The image of me taking a free kick is world renowned and instantly recognizable."[3]

Scoring off a free kick is a skill that is spreading. The World Cup saw a high of nine goals off free kicks in 2002 and six more in 2006. When Beckham scored a free kick goal in a 1–0 win against Ecuador at the 2006 World Cup, he became just the fifth player in history to score twice on free kicks in the World Cup.

Not all of Beckham's historic goals have come

off free kicks. His goal from midfield while on the move in a game against Wimbledon in 1996 remains one of Beckham's most memorable.

The three female leading roles (left to right) Shaznay Lewis, Keira Knightley, and Parminder Nagra arrive at the premiere of the film, *Bend It Like Beckham*, in London.

The FA Premier League gave out a series of awards in 2003 at the conclusion of ten seasons in its current format. The 10 Seasons Awards included a "Goal of the Decade," which went to Beckham's goal against Wimbledon.

More than 10,000 Premier League goals had been scored to that point, but Beckham's stood out as the best. Beckham combined both the power in his leg and the ability to control the height of the flight of the ball to loop it over goalie Neil Sullivan's head.

David Beckham officially unveiled his new personal logo at the adidas Global Headquarters in Germany in 2004. The logo design was inspired by Beckham's trademark free kicks.

"Goals are what football is all about, but sometimes the way a goal is scored makes it all the better," Premier League chief executive Richard Scudamore said. "David Beckham's strike was something special and arguably announced him as one of the Premier League's emerging talents of that time."[4]

More than 700,000 people voted for the award.

"I was very pleased to have been nominated for Goal of the Decade, but to win this award is a huge honor," Beckham said. "I am very proud; it means a great deal to me that fans all over the world have voted for me. That goal at Selhurst Park was a memorable moment for me; one that I will never forget."[5]

With their votes, the fans showed it was a goal they could not forget.

Manchester United's Teddy Sheringham (left) and David Beckham celebrate with the trophy after United beat Bayern Munich 2–1 to win the UEFA Champions League final in Barcelona on May 26, 1999.

7
ONE OF THE BEST

The Union of European Football Associations Champions League gathered in Monaco in the summer of 1999 for its annual awards dinner. David Beckham was not only honored as Midfielder of the Year but also, more significantly, as the Most Valuable Player.

Teammate Jaap Stam was Defender of the Year, and Alex Ferguson was Coach of the Year, giving Manchester United four awards following its treble. Beckham's award established him as the top player in Europe that season. Managers of the twenty-four teams that reached the Champions League voted on the award.

With certain exceptions, the question of who the best player is in a sport at any given time is often open to debate. An Internet poll featuring more than 12,000

Inter Milan's Portuguese ace Luis Figo (right) was named FIFA World Player of the Year in 2001, one spot ahead of Beckham.

votes from sixty countries was conducted by Megasoccer.com late in 2001. Beckham was named as the top player in the world in that poll, which awarded the Western Union MVP Award.

Beckham, however, came up just short of ever landing the most prestigious world player of the year award. FIFA has named the top three players in the world as part of its World Player of the Year honors since 1991. FIFA twice named Beckham as the second-best player in the world. In 1999, he ranked behind only Rivaldo of Brazil. In 2001, he was listed behind Luis Figo of Portugal.

"He was voted the second-best player in the world, but there's even more in him still," England team manager Kevin Keegan said while preparing for Euro 2000. "He's a big-match player as he's proved on numerous occasions."[1]

Beckham and Figo often played the same position, right midfield, and they eventually became teammates at Real Madrid.

"I think once people saw I was coming to Real Madrid, they said I was going to replace Figo out on the right," Beckham said. "Well, that never

> "I want to be on the same **team** as **Figo** because he is one of the world's **best** players, and to be on the same **team** as him would be a **great honor.**"

entered my head. I want to be on the same team as Figo because he is one of the best crossers in the world, one of the world's best players, and to be on the same team as him would be a great honor."[2]

The respect Beckham receives goes beyond a comparison with the best players of today. When FIFA prepared to celebrate its 100th anniversary in 2004, it turned to perhaps the most famous soccer player of all-time, Pelé, to help it honor the game's greats.

Beckham (left) holds his UEFA Awards trophy for Most Valuable Player in 1999. Beckham also received a second award for Best Midfielder.

Pelé was asked to choose the 100 greatest living soccer players. He wound up choosing 125 instead.

"Everyone has their own favorite 100 players, and I just tried to make as few mistakes as possible," Pelé said. "They asked me to pick 50 current players and 50 retired players from a short list of 300, but I could not manage that so I have picked 50 current and 75 former players."[3]

Beckham was one of seven English players on Pelé's list, joining Keegan, Bobby Charlton, Gordon Banks, Gary Lineker, Alan Shearer, and Michael Owen.

Figo, Beckham's Real Madrid teammate, agreed that he belonged on a list of the game's best players ever.

"David Beckham is a monster of soccer."

"David Beckham is a monster of soccer," Figo said. "He is not only in the current elite, he will go in history as one of the best of all times."[4]

8

NATIONAL TEAM

England took the field against Greece on October 6, 2001, needing a win or a tie to qualify as one of the thirty-two countries that would compete in the 2002 FIFA World Cup in South Korea and Japan.

Dick Jol, the referee from Holland, angered the Greek team at times by calling the match closely, not allowing for overly physical play. Part of the concern was that each foul called against Greece meant that England could turn to its captain, David Beckham, to take a free kick. Beckham, however, struggled with the plentiful opportunities that day, and Greece carried a 2–1 lead into extra time.

The teams reached the final minute of the time that was added onto the ninety-minute game for injuries and other stoppages. England's Teddy Sheringham got up from being fouled outside the Greek penalty area and, with Beckham struggling, got ready to take the kick himself. Beckham stepped up and said he was ready to take the shot.

Beckham curled the free kick from right to left, sending it beyond the reach of Greek goalkeeper Antonis Nikopoolidis' outstretched right hand and high into the net.

"One had to go in," Beckham said. "I had quite a few free kicks and was disappointed with most of them."[1]

England captain David Beckham (7) celebrates with his team after qualifying for the World Cup finals in 2001.

England's Leaders

Only two men served as captain of England's soccer team in international competition more often than David Beckham. Bobby Moore was captain for 90 games from 1963 to 1973. Bryan Robson was captain for 65 games from 1982 to 1991. Beckham served as captain 58 times, beginning in 2000, before stepping down following the 2006 World Cup.

Through 2007, Beckham was fifth all-time with 99 caps for England. Peter Shilton led with 125, followed by Moore with 108, Bobby Charlton with 106, and Billy Wright with 105.

Charlton, the man who ran the soccer schools that helped propel Beckham to stardom, was the all-time leading goal scorer for England with 49. Beckham is 22nd on the list with 17 goals.

Sven-Goran Eriksson, England's coach, was impressed that Beckham did not hesitate to take the shot on an otherwise tough day.

"You could see he wanted really, really hard to win this game, and he showed once again that he is such a big captain because he took his chance," Eriksson said.[2]

The result of the goal was just a 2–2 deadlock, but it was good for one of the most glorious ties in English soccer history. England took the spot it earned in the World Cup and advanced all the way to the quarter-finals as one of the last eight teams in contention for the title.

The goal was a highlight in one of the most amazing international careers ever produced by a player from England. Beckham is one of only seven players with at least ninety international caps for England. A cap occurs when a player plays a game for the national team. He started

eight of those games and served as captain for fifty-eight.

Bobby Moore, Bobby Charlton, and other members of the England 1966 World Cup team pose at the training ground at Roehampton, England.

Beckham got started in international play by playing nine times with England's Under-21 team from 1994 to 1996. Beckham was first capped by coach Glen Hoddle for a September 1996 game against Moldova. He scored for the first time in 1998 during a World Cup game against Colombia.

The first chance to play in a World Cup came in 1998. Beckham played in every qualifying match the year before to help England qualify for the tournament in France. Hoddle had questioned Beckham's concentration in preparation for the tournament and did not have him in the starting lineup for either of the first two games. Beckham started the third game, against Colombia, and scored on a long free kick in the 2–0 win.

England had advanced as one of sixteen teams in the elimination round, but what happened next left Beckham facing strong criticism from media and fans at home. Argentina's Diego Simeone fouled Beckham, who then kicked at Simeone, striking him on the calf. Simeone later admitted that he embellished his reaction to the kick to draw attention to it and joined with teammates in urging on the referee, who issued Beckham a red card for the unsportsmanlike action. The red card meant an ejection. Playing a man short, England still managed to tie Argentina. However, England lost in a shootout and was eliminated from the World Cup.

Beckham needed time to gradually prove himself as a leader capable of controlling his temper.

Beckham needed time to gradually prove himself as a leader capable of controlling his temper. His performances with Manchester United, while still competing for England, boosted his reputation.

Kevin Keegan resigned as England's coach in October 2000. Peter Taylor was coaching the team on

David Beckham (right) receives a red card during England's match against Argentina in the 1998 World Cup in France.

World Cup

The pageantry that accompanies the FIFA World Cup is like no other sporting event in the world. Fans of the world's most popular sporting event travel across continents and traverse hemispheres in order to cheer on their country's "football" teams. And they bring with them paint for their faces, flags to wave in the stands, cheers from the homeland, and money to spend.

When South Africa hosts the 2010 World Cup, the eyes of the world will be directed to the African nation. When France hosted the World Cup in 1998, 37 billion fans watched on television. The championship match had a television audience of 1.3 billion viewers worldwide. At the stadiums, 2.7 million fans took in the 64 matches.

The World Cup was first conducted in the 1930s, when it was held three times.

an interim basis a month later when he made Beckham captain for a friendly (non-tournament game) against Italy in 2000.

Sven-Goran Eriksson took over as coach of the English national team and kept Beckham in place as captain. Together, the new coach and captain led England to improved performances in international play.

England won five games, had two ties, and lost one to tie Germany for the top record in Group 9 during qualifying for the 2002 World Cup. The five-team, double round-robin play included a 5–1 win by England against Germany in Munich.

When England followed up the win against Germany in September with the key draw against Greece in October, Beckham was voted Sports Personality of the Year for 2001 by the British Broadcasting Company (BBC). Beckham also finished second to Portugal's

Luis Figo in voting for the FIFA World Player of the Year.

England opened the World Cup the next summer by playing to a 2–2 tie with Sweden. Beckham then scored the game's only goal on a penalty kick late in the first half of a 1–0 win against Argentina. Those two efforts helped England tie Sweden and beat out Argentina for the chance to become the two teams to advance out of a four-team pool that also included Nigeria.

Beckham (left) displays the 2001 BBC Sports Personality of the Year Award, while Manchester United manager Alex Ferguson holds the lifetime achievement award.

Sweden and England wound up among the sixteen teams that played elimination games to determine the champion. England needed just five minutes to start the scoring and got all of its goals in the first half of a 3–0 win against Denmark. In the quarterfinals, England jumped in front again midway through the first half but lost to Brazil, 2–1. Brazil went on from its quarterfinal rally to add two more victories and win the World Cup.

Beckham was still captain when it became time to qualify for the 2006 World Cup. He made sure that England qualified more comfortably this time around. Beckham scored the second goal in 2–0 wins against Wales and Azerbaijan during qualifying. England advanced by going 8–1–1 to win Group 6 and was ranked as the number-two team overall going into the Cup in Germany.

Going into the World Cup with such high expectations meant winning was not always enough. Beckham's free kick led to Paraguay's Carlos Gamarra putting the ball in his own goal less than three minutes into the competition, and England won its opener, 1–0. Beckham assisted both goals in a 2–0 win against Trinidad & Tobago as England clinched its spot in the round-of-sixteen elimination portion of the event in the least possible time.

Questions were raised in the English media about whether the team as a whole—and Beckham in particular—were playing up to potential following a 2–2 tie with Sweden to complete Group B pool play.

Beckham battled an illness before the first elimination game but still scored on a free kick in the second half to beat Ecuador, 1–0, and put England in the quarterfinals. Following his goal, Beckham vomited. He wound up having to be treated for dehydration.

"I didn't feel well before the game, but I thought I would be fine, and in the first half I felt fine," Beckham said, "but the sickness continued in the second half."[3]

> Going into the **World Cup** with such **high** expectations meant **winning** was not always **enough**.

The win left Beckham feeling better in light of the negative reactions in England following group play.

"It was nice to silence a few people who have been critical," he said. "I can handle my criticism, and I'll prove them wrong. It was a great feeling to get a goal and put us into the quarterfinal."[4]

John Terry, the Chelsea player who would eventually succeed Beckham as captain, was impressed by the effort.

"Becks has been banging them in in training all week and he was fantastic today," Terry said after the win. "Of course everyone looks at his free kicks and his passing, but he tackles back and works hard for the team. He is brilliant, and sometimes it goes unnoticed."[5]

The excitement of the win against Ecuador, however, was soon followed by disappointment against Portugal. Beckham was injured early in the second half. High-level soccer rules require a player to be out for the remainder of the game once a substitute replaces him. Beckham's injury led to a substitution. All Beckham could do was watch in anguish as the teams remained tied, 0–0, through overtime.

Beckham watched as the game moved to a penalty kick shootout where each team gets to have five different players attempt penalty shots from 11 meters (12 yards) out. Portugal made three of its shots. Although the goalkeeper is generally at a distinct disadvantage in soccer shootouts, England could only convert one shot.

Portugal moved on to the semifinals of a World Cup tournament that was ultimately won by Italy.

Beckham's World Cup was likely done anyway because of the injuries that sent him to the sideline against Portugal. He suffered a tear in his right Achilles' tendon and ligament damage in his left knee, putting him out of action for six weeks.

With England out of the competition, Beckham made an announcement the next day. The tears that were difficult to fight off during the Portugal game were now flowing as Beckham announced that he was stepping down as team captain.

"On 15 November 2000, Peter Taylor gave me the greatest honor of my career in making me the captain of England, fulfilling my childhood dream," Beckham said. "It has been an honor and a privilege to have captained our country, and I want to stress that I wish to continue to play for England and look forward to helping both the new captain and Steve McLaren any way I can."[6]

McLaren, who replaced Eriksson following the World Cup, saw things differently. When he announced his national team in August, he left Beckham off the roster.

"Of course everyone **looks** at his **free kicks** and his **passing,** but he tackles back and works **hard** for the **team. He** is **brilliant,** and sometimes it goes **unnoticed.**"

9

REAL MADRID

David Beckham returned to Old Trafford, home of Manchester United, for a game as a member of Real Madrid in 2007. Looking back on the early stages of his professional career, Beckham was thankful that he had played for coach Alex Ferguson.

"I would not be the player and the person I am today without him," Beckham said. "It's been well documented that we had our ups and downs, of course once or twice. But you know I owe almost everything to him. Obviously I had strong parents and family behind me. Without him giving me the actual opportunity to go into this team and be part of the club, I wouldn't be the player I am today. I would not have won and have achieved a lot of things that I have done."[1]

Beckham saw the trip back to Old Trafford as a bit of a disappointment. A knee injury kept him from playing for Real Madrid in a Champions League game against his old team, Manchester United.

"I am disappointed because one thing I've looked forward to doing for four years since I left United was to go back to the stadium," he said. "I never had a chance to say goodbye—it all happened so quickly, my move to Madrid."[2]

Just as Beckham's move to the United States in 2007 came after years of speculation, rumors of Real Madrid's interest in obtaining Beckham started long before the move took place. Each wave of rumors was followed by strong denials.

The move away from Manchester United, the team he had cheered for as a young boy, became a possibility largely because of the deteriorating relationship with Ferguson. In the years following the treble, Ferguson became more critical of Beckham's play.

Ferguson gave the appearance of being bothered by the fame of the Beckhams. There were problems when Beckham missed a game to tend to his son Brooklyn, who was ill, while Victoria Beckham was off at a fashion event. Similarly, a visit with the queen— when Ferguson thought Beckham should be working to rehabilitate from an injury—did not go over well.

Victoria Beckham, wife of England soccer team captain David Beckham, holds their son Romeo during a 2004 match between England and France in Lisbon, Portugal.

Following a 2–0 loss to Arsenal in the FA Cup on February 15, 2003, Ferguson harshly criticized Beckham in the locker room. This time, Beckham argued back, angering his coach. Ferguson stepped toward Beckham and kicked a boot in his direction. The boot, as soccer shoes are called in England, flew up and struck Beckham in the head, cutting him above the left eyebrow. Teammates had to hold Beckham back when he tried to go after his coach.

Team officials tried to keep the story quiet, but news of the "flying boot" spread. Days later, both Beckham and Ferguson said they put the incident behind them, but within months, Beckham's career with Manchester United was finished. Ferguson no longer denied kicking the boot. He only said that he did not expect it to hit Beckham in the head.

"It was a freakish accident," Ferguson said. "If I tried it one hundred or a million times, it couldn't happen again. If I could, I would have carried on playing."[3]

Beckham referred to the incident as "just one of those things."[4]

Real Madrid, which in recent years had already made a tradition of acquiring some of the best and most famous players in the world, was an upcoming opponent for Manchester United. This only served to increase the number of stories speculating on Beckham's future.

> Beckham had **signed** a **three-year** contract with Manchester United, making him the **highest-paid** soccer player in the **world**.

Despite missing part of the 2001–02 season with a broken bone in his left foot, Beckham had signed a new, three-year contract with Manchester United after the season, making him the highest-paid soccer player

Alex Ferguson

Alex Ferguson was granted knighthood in the United Kingdom following Manchester United's treble of the Premiership, FA Cup, and European Cup during the 1998–99 season.

While the title is symbolic only, it brings prestige and membership in an elite club. Film director Steven Spielberg, Microsoft founder Bill Gates, and singer Placido Domingo have received honorary knighthoods, although they cannot use the word "Sir" because they are not British. Paul McCartney of Beatles fame, however, is British and does get the "Sir" honors.

Ferguson, of Scottish ancestry, did not take a step back after being knighted. Instead, he went on to coach Manchester United to trebles in both 1999–2000, and 2000–01. That's three trebles in a row.

in the world. Any move to another team would have to come with Manchester United's approval.

When Ferguson seemed to have enough of the relationship with his star player following the "flying boot," the time was right for Real Madrid to make its move.

Beckham's status as the highest-paid player was not a problem for Real Madrid owner Florentino Perez. He was already paying the second- and third-largest contracts to Zinedine Zidane and Ronaldo. The task was negotiating a transfer fee with Manchester United, which wound up accepting a reported 35 million euros [approximately $41.3 million at the time] to relinquish its rights to Beckham.

Real Madrid was lacking depth and a strong defensive presence, but Perez had managed to put together a team of the world's biggest stars. Raul, Luis Figo, and Roberto Carlos were also part of the lineup, giving

A Spanish newspaper headline screamed "The Sixth Galactic," referring to Real Madrid's 2003 signing of Beckham.

the Spanish professional team seven of the last eight FIFA World Players of the Year at one point. The roster also included the captains of England, France (Zidane), Spain (Raul), and Portugal (Figo). In Spain, the collection of stars became known as "Los Galacticos."

Real Madrid had already replaced Manchester United as the world's richest soccer club the year before obtaining Beckham, according to World Soccer magazine.

"We're content providers like a film studio," Real Madrid director of marketing Jose Angel Sanchez said.

"Having a team with Zidane in it is like having a movie with Tom Cruise."[5]

Instead of cutting into its wealth by paying the transfer free and a large contract to Beckham, Real Madrid made more money. Just as with its earlier signings of other stars, Real Madrid more than offset what it spent because of increases in attendance, television rights fees, and jersey sales. In 2003, with just half the calendar year to work with, Real Madrid sold one million soccer shirts with the name "Beckham" on them.

> **"Real Madrid excited me. They're a great club—and this was the only team that excited me."**

The magnitude of the Real Madrid club captivated Beckham.

"This was the only team I wanted to come to," Beckham said. "Real Madrid excited me. They're a great club—massive club—and this was the only team that excited me."[6]

Beckham said Real Madrid was a team and not just a collection of stars.

"They play amazing football, exciting football, but effective football as well," he said. "Playing against them at Bernabeu was a very, very difficult game. I think the first half the football that they played was absolutely amazing, and astonishing. For me now

David Beckham celebrates after scoring for Real Madrid against Mallorca at Bernabeu Stadium in Madrid, Spain, in 2003.

being part of that—hopefully being part of that—is a very proud time for me."[7]

Before long, Beckham fit right in.

"David has already shown he fits in well," Zidane said after their first game together. "It's a bit early to say, but things look good already."[8]

Beckham concentrated on trying to show he was part of the group.

"Me coming to Real Madrid is not about me coming to be the main star," Beckham said. "It's joining a whole team of stars."[9]

The expectations were incredibly high.

"Every year we raise the bar at Real," Zidane said. "First there was Figo, then me, then Ronaldo. With Beckham coming and with the strength of this team as a whole, the objective will be to win both (the Spanish La Liga and European Champions League) this season."[10]

Beckham scored his first goal for Real Madrid during a 2–0 win in an exhibition game against FC Tokyo in Japan. When it came time to make his home debut, Beckham did not disappoint the fans in Madrid. Playing in the final of the Spanish Super Cup, which serves as the build-up to the beginning of league play, Real Madrid had lost the first part of the two-game final, 2–1, at Mallorca.

Back at home at Santiago Bernabeu Stadium, Real Madrid needed to win the second leg by at least two goals to have a higher total score and win the Cup. Raul scored just before halftime, and Ronaldo scored early in the second half for the necessary 2–0 lead. Beckham then helped put Real Mallorca away by using a header to convert a pass from Ronaldo into his first home goal for Real Madrid.

"I've said playing out there was going to be a special occasion and a special feeling but it can't get any better than that for a debut," Beckham said.[11]

Beckham's foot and his free kicks may be famous, but he is not exactly known for using his head.

"To get a headed-in goal is special for me," he said. "I don't know when I last scored one."[12]

The Super Cup, the seventh that Real Madrid won, added to the anticipation of the special times ahead. The 2003–04 league results, however, were unable to match up to the expectations. Beckham's personal statistics were fine for a midfielder, but the team settled into a

Zinedine Zidane

As popular and far-reaching as David Beckham's soccer exploits have become on the world stage, he has never won the FIFA World Player of the Year title.

In addition to having a cool-sounding name, Beckham's former teammate on Real Madrid had quite the collection of honors. France's Zinedine Zidane was named World Player of the Year in 1998, 2000, and 2002. He was a top three finisher for the award on three other occasions.

A member of the French national team, he had been nicknamed Zizou. In order for Zidane to join "Los Galacticos" in 2001, Real Madrid had to pay a transfer sum of $64.5 million to Juventus of Italy. It was the highest fee ever paid. Real Madrid paid 35 million euros (approximately $41.3 million at the time) in transfer fees to Manchester United for Beckham.

disappointing fourth place in La Liga. Counting friendlies and Championship League play, Beckham scored five goals in his first sixteen games with Real Madrid.

"I think in the beginning, he was under pressure because people expected a little bit more," Figo said. "I think he answered all those questions and is doing a great job for Real Madrid. He is a really important player for us and has made us even stronger this year."[13]

> **"I think in the beginning, he was under pressure because people expected a little bit more."**

He could not make Real Madrid strong enough. The team was the highest scoring in La Liga but still lost ten times. Playing in the Champions League, Real Madrid was knocked out before the final four, losing in the quarterfinals.

Real Madrid improved its La Liga performance in Beckham's second season. The team won twenty-five times and added five draws while losing just eight times to finish with eighty points, good for second place but still four points behind league champion FC Barcelona. Juventus sent Real Madrid home in the first round of elimination play from the Champions League.

Beckham led La Liga in assists during the 2005–06 season, and Real Madrid managed to remain in second place, but the gap behind FC Barcelona was widening.

Barcelona finished with an 82–70 lead in standings points when Real Madrid dipped to twenty wins. Real Madrid made the cut to sixteen teams in the Champions League, but then immediately lost to Arsenal and was eliminated prior to the quarterfinals for the second straight season.

By his fourth and final season with Real Madrid, Beckham's status was not quite the same in Spain. His playing time was dwindling, and when he did play, the team tended to struggle. Jose Antonio Reyes took over as the player who started most often at right midfield. Once the announcement of Beckham's contract with the Los Angeles Galaxy was made January 11, 2007, Real Madrid coach Fabio Capello said Beckham would spend the rest of his time on the bench.

Capello quickly reversed that opinion, but injuries also minimized Beckham's time on the field.

"Often you make mistakes," Capello said. "If he is in a good physical condition, on form and mentally right, he can be part of the team. I have no friends or enemies. I have a squad of players, and I have to pick the players I think are best."[14]

Real Madrid was remaining competitive in third place in La Liga but well behind the top two teams, Barcelona and FC Sevilla. The mystique that came with the signing of "Los Galacticos" was also disappearing. In early March 2007, Roberto Carlos said he would follow Beckham out the door. Carlos arrived at

Real Madrid in 1996 and was part of three Spanish and three Champions League titles before the others arrived.

"I don't deserve more suffering," Carlos said after his turnover allowed Bayern Munich's Roy Makaay to score just eleven seconds into a Champions League match that Real Madrid lost, 2–1. "I've been at this club eleven years, in which seven-and-a-half years we won many things, but we lose one game and all the fault has landed on me. I don't accept this."[15]

The time had come for Beckham to leave a professional team behind for the second time in his career. Although his Real Madrid squad had won far more often than it had lost and had created unprecedented interest and income, it had failed to produce the expected number of championships.

The task ahead would again be an odd one for a competitive athlete. The Los Angeles Galaxy will seek championships with Beckham in the lineup, but his role is again tied to the economics of his team and league as much as his ability to win games.

Few players have ever possessed the rare combination of talent and personality to be prepared to take on such a task. Just in case there was any doubt, Beckham brought out his old flare for the dramatic before his arrival in the United States.

10
ARRIVING IN STYLE

David Beckham made it to the United States on July 12, 2007. Clearly, his arrival was eagerly awaited by soccer fans and the media.

More than one hundred media organizations were at the airport when the Beckhams arrived in Los Angeles. Fans gathered behind metal barriers just to watch David and Victoria walk by. The media group was several times larger the next day for Beckham's first press conference as an actual member of the Los Angeles Galaxy team.

The time leading up to and immediately following Beckham's signing with the Galaxy included some of the roughest stretches of his career.

David Beckham and his wife Victoria arrive at the Los Angeles International Airport in July 2007 as he prepared to start his career with the Los Angeles Galaxy.

By the time he was ready to leave Europe for North America, Beckham was back on top of his game. Beckham fought his way back into the lineup at Real Madrid and for England and helped both teams become more successful in the process.

Beckham returned to the England lineup in time for the opening of the new Wembley Stadium in a friendly game against Brazil on June 1. "It is always nice to have the support of the fans and I have had that throughout my career," Beckham said. "It was amazing out there for me. Things are in the past now and I am happy

> **The time leading up to and immediately following Beckham's signing with the Galaxy included some of the roughest stretches of his career.**

to have been part of this historic occasion."[1]

Beckham was more than just a member of the team again. He was a major factor. Beckham not only started, but he also assisted in three of the four goals in his first two games—a 1–1 tie with Brazil and a 3–0 victory in Estonia. "I have always felt that I have had to play for my place and I have always done that in every team that I have played for."[2]

In his first national team game since the World Cup in 2006, Beckham was greeted by a standing

Real Madrid

David Beckham left the team he cheered for as a youngster (Manchester United) to play for Real Madrid, the team that FIFA called "the best club of the 20th century."

Beckham ended a four-year stay with Real Madrid by helping Los Blancos (The Whites) win their thirtieth La Liga title in June 2007. Real Madrid had won the crown the season prior to Beckham's arrival but couldn't find its way back to the top until Beckham's final game with the club.

Only weeks before Beckham was set to make his journey to the United States to play for the Los Angeles Galaxy, he helped Real Madrid reach the pinnacle again. Tom Cruise, the movie actor who lives in Los Angeles, came to watch his friend play in his finale with Real Madrid. Beckham's ankle injury prevented him from tallying any goals or assists, but Real Madrid defeated Mallorca 3–1 to clinch the La Liga title.

ovation from the sellout crowd at Wembley. His free kick set up a goal by John Terry for a 1–0 lead.

With Beckham in the lineup June 6, England was too much for Estonia during a Euro 2008 qualifying match in Tallinn. Beckham assisted goals by Peter Crouch and Michael Owen to turn a 1–0 lead into a comfortable 3–0 win. From all the way out on the right sideline, Beckham crossed a ball to Crouch for a header and goal.

Before Beckham returned to play for England, he had made his way back into the Real Madrid lineup and produced impressive results. When Beckham's signing with the Galaxy was first announced, Real Madrid coach Fabio Capello said he would not use Beckham in any more games. Beckham was not even welcome to train with the team at times.

Beckham kept working and Capello eventually changed his mind, calling the star midfielder back into play to lead the team on a surge from fourth place to first place in the Spanish League standings. "A major fault of mine this season was not recognizing Beckham's potential," Capello said after the last game.[3] Real Madrid lost just once in seventeen games after Beckham returned to the lineup in May, winning eleven times and playing to a tie five times. "I admit I got that wrong," Capello said. "I think bringing him back was one of the most important influences on the way we have come back and claimed the title."[4]

In his last eleven appearances from February to June, the team won eight times and had three ties.

Real Madrid finally had the championship that had been expected throughout Beckham's time there.

When it was all over, Real Madrid finally had the championship that had been expected throughout Beckham's time there. Capello was even talking about ways to still keep Beckham on the team rather than have him leave for the United States.

Real Madrid was already eliminated from the Champions League and six points behind first-place FC Barcelona in the Spanish League when Beckham returned to the lineup. The results were immediate.

Beckham bent in a free kick for a goal in a 2–1 win over Real Sociedad in his first game back. He left the team again for six weeks because of a knee injury, then returned to the lineup to assist on the game-winner in a 2–1 win over Valencia. Real Madrid took off on an eight-game winning streak, averaging three goals per game.

Another knee injury during a 1–1 draw against Getafe on March 4, 2007, also sent him to the sidelines.

Real Madrid needed a win on the final day of the season at home at Santiago Bernebeu Stadium. It got the win despite Beckham suffering what was soon to become a very famous sprain to his left ankle during the second half. Jose Antonio Reyes replaced Beckham and played a prominent role as Real Madrid rallied to score three goals to beat Real Mallorca, 3–1. The win meant that even FC Barcelona's 5–1 romp over Gimnastic Tarragone could not keep Real Madrid from a first-place finish. "It's been an incredible experience," Beckham said on his final night with Real Madrid. "All I remember now are the great things. Winning this puts everything else to bed."[5]

Before leaving Spain, Beckham had provided one more example of flare for the dramatic. "This is a perfect ending and I will always miss Bernabeu," Beckham said. "It was amazing to have my family here with me. They have been with me for four years and felt the ups and downs, and they feel the euphoria tonight. It meant the world to have everyone here that supported me throughout my career."[6]

Beckham was no longer a member of Real Madrid. He was once again part of the England national team during the times when he could break away from his new club. It was time to prepare for his debut with the Los Angeles Galaxy.

Beckham's arrival in California brought with it much anticipation for his first game with the Galaxy. Beckham wrapped things up in Europe and headed for the United States even though his sprained ankle was not healed.

After handling public appearances and press conferences as a member of the Galaxy, Beckham still was unable to do any serious practice work because of the swelling in his ankle. Fans and the media were waiting to hear when he would actually play in a game.

> **Beckham** was no longer a member of **Real Madrid.** It was time to prepare for his **debut** with the **Los Angeles Galaxy.**

Even following the announcement that Beckham's Galaxy debut would come June 21 in an ESPN-televised Saturday night game against Chelsea, there was much speculation about whether he was healthy enough to play. The speculation and the questions continued through the days leading up to the game.

Beckham sat on the bench for the entire first half and the first twenty minutes of the second half. Even there, he was the source of as much attention as the action on the field in Chelsea's 1–0 victory.

Eventually Beckham got up to began stretching, disappeared into the locker room area briefly and returned ready to play. After six months worth of anticipation, Beckham entered the Galaxy lineup with twelve minutes to play. Cameras flashed all around the packed 27,000-seat Home Depot Center.

"The atmosphere is incredible," Beckham said. "It made me feel a little bit embarrassed at times."[7] Chelsea coach Jose Mourinho understood the significance of the moment. "The objective was just for him to be on the pitch and give the people the dessert they were looking for," Mourinho said.[8]

There was more excitement created by the scene and the moment than by Beckham's play in the first brief appearance. One scary moment added to the drama. Chelsea's Steve Sidwell attempted to tackle Beckham sliding at the ball and the taped ankle. Although there was contact and Beckham wound up on the ground, he said he didn't take much of a hit. "I saw him coming and I jumped just in time so my foot wasn't planted when he hit me," Beckham said.[9]

Beckham, who still needed time to recover and get himself back in top game shape, was only down briefly. He bounced back up and there was much more Galaxy

Beckham, with his new team the Los Angeles Galaxy, dribbles the ball during a 2007 World Series of Football exhibition game against Chelsea at the Home Depot Center in Carson, California.

Posh Spice

The summer of 2007 proved to be exciting for Victoria Beckham, as well as her husband, David.

Victoria, Posh Spice from the pop group the Spice Girls, was the subject of many high-profile television interviews. She also wound up with her own reality television show, coinciding with David's arrival to play soccer for the Los Angeles Galaxy.

Mixed in with all the fame surrounding the soccer field, Victoria's profile rose with talks of a reunion of the Spice Girls.

The 2007–2008 Spice Girls reunion World Tour took the group back to England and Spain. They named the Boeing 747 on which they flew "Spice One."

soccer for fans to eagerly await in the remainder of the season for a struggling team.

"After this game, we've got a lot of season left," Beckham said. "This is where the hard work starts. It's not hopefully just about the exhibition game and getting fans here for this game. It's about getting the fans here for every game that we play."[10]

His first year as an MLS player brought plenty of attention, but injuries forced Beckham to the sideline. He made his MLS debut with the Galaxy on August 9, when he entered as a substitute in the second half of a 1–0 loss to D.C. United.

On August 15 in a SuperLiga match against D.C. United, Beckham earned his first start. In that game, he was also named captain, received his first yellow card, and scored his first goal on a free kick. He also assisted on the

Galaxy's goal in the second half to help the team to a 2–0 win.

His first MLS start was on August 18, when 66,237 spectators filled Giants Stadium in New Jersey. Beckham had two assists in a 5–4 loss to Red Bull New York. The event set a Giants Stadium record for an MLS game.

Beckham's lifestyle allowed him to be in London the following week to play in England's match against Germany. After the game ended, it was back to Los Angeles for the Galaxy's match the next day.

A knee injury in the SuperLiga final on August 29 resulted in Beckham being sidelined for six weeks. He played as a second-half substitute in the Galaxy's 1–1 tie with the Red Bull New York on October 18, then did the same in a season-ending loss to the Chicago Fire. In his rookie regular-season in MLS, Beckham played in five matches and had no goals and two assists.

Beckham made good on his promise to continue to represent England in international competition. On November 21, 2007, he earned his 99th cap in a loss to Croatia that eliminated England from the Euro Cup 2008 finals. Upon playing in his next international game, Beckham will become just the fifth player ever to earn 100 caps for England.

CHRONOLOGY

1975 Born on May 2 in Leytonstone, England, the second of Ted and Sandra Beckham's three children.

1983 Scores more than 100 goals for the Ridgeway Rovers of the Enfield District League.

1986 Attends the Bobby Charlton Soccer Schools as an 11-year-old.

1987 Invited to Manchester United training sessions and practices, and serves as a mascot at a Manchester United game.

1988 Gets moved up from the 13-year-old team to an older group at the Bobby Charlton Soccer Schools.

1989 Signs schoolboy forms committing to Manchester United on the day of his 14th birthday.

1991 Signs a youth contract with Manchester United as a 16-year-old.

1992 Scores a goal in the final as Manchester United wins the FA Youth Cup.

1993 Helps Manchester United finish as runner-up in the FA Youth Cup.

Helps Manchester United reserve team win the FA Youth Cup, and plays his first full game with the top team.	**1994**
Scores his first Premier League goal with Manchester United.	**1995**
Helps Manchester United win both the Premier League and FA Cup. In a game against Wimbledon, Beckham scores a goal by looping from midfield over the goalkeeper's head for the first of what would become many goals that led to the movie, *Bend It Like Beckham*. Beckham is capped for the first time versus Moldova.	**1996**
Wins EA Young Player of the Year award and finishes second in voting for EA Player of the Year. Begins dating Victoria Adams, also known as "Posh Spice," from the Spice Girls music group.	**1997**
Scores his first goal after being capped in a World Cup game versus Colombia. Later receives a red card in a World Cup game versus Argentina, and England loses the match in a shootout to be eliminated.	**1998**

1999	Marries Victoria Adams and helps Manchester United win the treble. Champions League names Beckham Midfielder of the Year and Most Valuable Player. Finishes as runner-up in FIFA World Player of the Year voting.
2000	Earns captain designation for England in a friendly versus Italy.
2001	Finishes as runner-up in FIFA World Player of the Year voting. Beckham named Sports Personality of the Year by the BBC.
2002	The movie *Bend It Like Beckham* is released in England.
2003	Suffers a cut above his eye when Manchester United coach Alex Ferguson kicks a soccer cleat at him in the locker room. Signs with Real Madrid. Shoots a commercial at the Home Depot Center, home of the Los Angeles Galaxy of MLS. The movie *Bend It Like Beckham* is released in the United States. Beckham's goal against Wimbledon in 1996 is named "Goal of the Decade" among 10,000 total goals by the FA Premier League.

Honored with his own logo from sponsor adidas.	**2004**
Plays for Real Madrid in a game versus the MLS All-Stars in Spain.	**2005**
Becomes the first player from England to score in three World Cups when he converted a free kick versus Ecuador. After losing to Portugal in the World Cup quarterfinals in a game in which he injured his knee, Beckham, 31, steps down from his role as captain of Team England. New Team England coach Steve McLaren leaves Beckham off the Team England roster. Beckham leads La Liga in assists for Real Madrid.	**2006**
Los Angeles Galaxy signs Beckham to a five-year contract. The deal for Beckham's services on the field is believed to be for $50 million; the total with marketing and promotional duties could reach $250 million. Beckham plays a key role in helping Real Madrid win the La Liga title in his final game with the team. Beckham returns to Team England to play in the opening game at the new Wembley Stadium. Plays in just five regular-season games with the Galaxy due to ankle and knee injuries.	**2007**

TITLES WON BY
DAVID BECKHAM'S TEAMS

1995–96—English Premier League Championship

1996—FA Cup

1996–97—English Premier League Championship

1998–99—English Premier League Championship

1999—FA Cup

1999—UEFA Champions League (1)

1999–2000—English Premier League Championship

2000–01—English Premier League Championship

2002–03—English Premier League Championship

2007—Spanish League

CHAPTER NOTES

Chapter 1. Coming to America

1. Grant Wahl, "Vend It Like Beckham," *Sports Illustrated*, January 22, 2007, p. 16-17.

2. Grant Wahl, "Anatomy of a blockbuster: The story behind the Beckham deal and the economics," *Sports Illustrated* Web site, January 17, 2007, <http://sportsillustrated.cnn.com/2007/writers/grant_wahl/01/17/beckham.qa/?cnn=yes> (February 11, 2007).

3. Ibid.

4. Beth Harris, "Beckham says U.S. soccer has 'huge potential,'" Associated Press story on MSNBC Web site, January 12, 2007, <http://www.msnbc.msn.com/id/16453485> (February 11, 2007).

5. Ibid.

6. "Global icon David Beckham signs with the Los Angeles Galaxy in landmark deal," Press release, MLS Web site, January 11, 2007, <http://web.mlsnet.com/news/mls_news.jsp?ymd=20070111&content_id=81619&vkey=pr_mls&fext=.jsp> (February 11, 2007).

7. Ibid.

8. "David Beckham statement on joining the Los Angeles Galaxy," Press release. MLS Web site, January 11, 2007, <http://web.mlsnet.com/news/mls_news.jsp?ymd=20070111&content_id=81599&vkey=pr_mls&fext=.jsp> (February 11, 2007).

9. Grant Wahl, "Anatomy of a blockbuster: The story behind the Beckham deal and the economics," *Sports Illustrated* Web site, January 17, 2007, <http://sportsillustrated.cnn.com/2007/writers/grant_wahl/01/17/beckham.qa/?cnn=yes> (February 11, 2007).

10. Ibid.

11. Ibid.

Chapter 2. Starting Early

1. "David Beckham Story," Bobby Charlton Soccer Schools and Sports Academy Web site, n.d., <http://www.bcssa.co.uk/david_beckham_story.php> (March 6, 2007).

2. Ibid.

Chapter 3. Professional Promotion

1. "Ryan Kidd interview," Preston North End Football Club Web site, n.d., <http://www.pnefc.premiumtv.co.uk/page/LegendsDetail/0,,10362~532152,00.html> (March 10, 2007).

2. Simon Hattenstone, "The greys of the Reds make me want to be old again," n.d., <http://blogs.guardian.co.uk/sport/2007/01/10/the _greys_of_the _reds_make_me.html> (March 9, 2007).

3. "Goal of the Decade: Beckham," Premier League Web site, n.d., <http://tenseasons. premierleague.com/index.jsp> (March 22, 2007).

Chapter 4. Celebrity Life

1. "Spice Girls make pop history," BBC Web site, October 29, 2000, <http://news.bbc.co.uk/ 2/hi/entertainment/997495.stm> (March 19, 2007).

2. Simon Moon, "This is Money: Beckham the worldwide brand," *thisismoney.co.uk*, June 8, 2006, <http://thisismoney.co.uk/news/special-report/ article.html?in_artice_id=409642&in_page_id=108> (March 19, 2007).

3. Ibid.

4. Ibid.

5. John Carlin, *White Angels: Beckham, Real Madrid, & the New Football*, Bloomsbury Publishing, New York, 2004, p. 68-69.

6. Ibid., p. 96.

Chapter 5. Triple Crown

1. "Barcelona: Quotes at a glance," BBC News Web site, May 27, 1999, <http://news.bbc.co.uk/ 2/hi/sport/football/353901.stm> (March 20, 2007).

2. "The Miracle of the Nou Camp," Manchester United Web site, n.d., <http://www.manutdzone.com /greatgames/greatgame1.html> (March 20, 2007).

3. Ibid.

4. "Beckham backs Man Utd to repeat treble," espn.com, March 8, 2007, <http://soccernet-akamai.espn.go.com/news/story?id=413240&cc=5901> (March 22, 2007).

Chapter 6. Bend It Like Beckham

1. "David Beckham quotes" Expert Football Web site, n.d., <http://expertfootball.com/players/beckham/quotes.php> (March 22, 2007).

2. "David Beckham gets own logo," Press release, adidas Web site, March 3, 2004, <http://www.press.adidas.com/DesktopDefault.aspx/tabid-16/94_read-1318/> (March 21, 2007).

3. Ibid.

4. "Goal of the Decade: Beckham," Premier League Web site, n.d., <http://tenseasons.premierleague.com/index.jsp> (March 22, 2007).

5. Ibid.

Chapter 7. One of the Best

1. "Beckham: I've never felt better," BBC Sport Web site, June 2, 2000, <http://news.bbc.co.uk/2/hi/euro2000/teams/england/774978.stm> (March 22, 2007).

2. John Carlin, *White Angels: Beckham, Real Madrid, & the New Football*, Bloomsbury Publishing, New York, 2004, p. 92.

3. "FIFA names greatest list," BBC Sport Web site, March 4, 2004, <http://news.bbc.co.uk/go/pr/fr/-/sport2/hi/football/3533833.stm> (March 22, 2007).

4. "Figo: 'Monster' Beckham," TheFA.com, February 18, 2004, <http://www.thefa.com/England/SeniorTeam/NewsAndFeatures/Postings/2004/02/England> (March 23, 2007).

Chapter 8. National Team

1. Stephen Wilson, "England, Italy, Russia qualify for World Cup," *CBC Sports*, October 6, 2001, <http://www.cbc.ca/sports/story/2001/10/06/worldcup011006.html> (March 16, 2007).

2. Ibid.

3. "I proved critics wrong – Beckham," *BBC Sports*. June 25, 2006, <http://news.bbc.co.uk/sport2/hi/football/world_cup_2006/teams/england/5103576.stm> (September 13, 2007).

4. Ibid.

5. Ibid.

6. "Beckham quits as England captain," BBC Sports. July 2, 2006, <http://news.bbc.co.uk/sport1/hi/football/world_cup_2006/teams/england/5138288.stm> (March 18, 2007).

Chapter 9. Real Madrid

1. "Beckham backs Man Utd to repeat treble," espn.com, March 8, 2007, <http://soccernet-akamai.espn.go.com/news/story?id=413240&cc=5901> (March 22, 2007).

2. Ibid.

3. "Beckham forgives Ferguson," BBC Sport Web site, February 19, 2003, <http://news.bbc.co.uk/sport/hi/football/teams/m/man_utd/2778353.stm> (March 23, 2007).

4. Ibid.

5. Martin Jacques, "Football's new world order," *Observer Sport Monthly*, June 6, 2004, <http://observer.guardian.co.uk/osm/story/0..1229700,00.html> (January 23, 2008).

6. John Carlin, *White Angels: Beckham, Real Madrid, & the New Football*, Bloomsbury Publishing, New York, 2004, p. 90.

7. Ibid., p. 91.

8. "David Beckham quotes" Expert Football Web site, n.d., <http://expertfootball.com/players/beckham/quotes.php> (March 22, 2007).

9. Carlin, p. 92.

10. "David Beckham quotes" Expert Football Web site, n.d., <http://expertfootball.com/players/beckham/quotes.php> (March 22, 2007).

11. "Becks the 'supercampeon'," TheFA.com, August 28, 2003, <http://www.thefa.com/England/SeniorTeam/NewsAndFeatures/Postings/2003/08/63269.htm> (March 23, 2007).

12. Ibid.

13. "Figo: 'Monster' Beckham," TheFA.com, February 18, 2004, <http://www.thefa.com/ England/SeniorTeam/NewsAndFeatures/Postings/ 2004/02/England> (March 23, 2007).

14. "Capello Admits Beckham Mistake," *The London Times*, January 27, 2007, <http://www.timesonline.co.uk/article/ 0,27-2569393,00.html> (February 12, 2007).

15. Paul Logothetis, "Carlos to leave Real Madrid," *Slam Sports*, March 9, 2007, <http://slam.canoe.ca/ Slam/Soccer/2007/03/09/3721453-ap.html> (March 23, 2007).

Chapter 10. Arriving in Style

1. Mark Isaacs, "Beckham Delighted," thefa.com, June 2, 2007, <http://www.thefa.com/ England/SeniorTeam/NewsAndFeatures/Postings/ 2007/06/EnglandBrazil_Beckham.htm> (August 1, 2007).

2. Ibid.

3. "Beckham limps off field in final game with Real Madrid," Associated Press story on espn.com, June 17, 2007, <http://soccernet.espn.go.com/ news/story?id=439478&cc=5901> (August 1, 2007).

4. "Real wins 30th title in heart-stopping finale," Reuters story on espn.com, June 17, 2007, <http://soccernet.espn.go.com/news/story?id=439426 &cc=5901> (August 1, 2007).

5. Douglas Robson, "Beckham bows out in Spain with Real Madrid title," *USA Today*, June 17, 2007, <http://www.usatoday.com/sports/soccer/2007-06-17-beckham-focus_N.htm> (August 1, 2007).

6. Ibid.

7. "Beckham's debut brief, but still a big deal," Associated Press story on msnbc.com. July 22, 2007, <http://www.msnbc.com/id/19891512> (August 1, 2007).

8. Ibid.

9. Ibid.

10. By Robert Falkoff, "Beckham LA ready to get crackin'," *MLSnet.com.* July 23, 2007, <http://ww2.mlsnet.com/news/team_news.jsp?ymd=20070723&content_id=107447&vkey=news_lag&fext=.jsp&team=t106> (August 1, 2007).

FURTHER READING

Carlin, John. *White Angels: Beckham, Real Madrid & the New Football*. New York: Bloomsbury, 2004.

Russell, Gwen. *Arise, Sir David Beckham*. London: J. Blake, 2007.

Beckham, David with Tom Watt. *Beckham: Both Feet on the Ground*. New York: HarperCollins, 2004.

Burns, Jimmy. *When Beckham Went to Spain: Power, Stardom, and Real Madrid*. London: Penguin, 2004.

INTERNET ADDRESSES

International soccer site

www.fifa.com

Los Angeles Galaxy team site

www.lagalaxy.com

Official David Beckham site

www.davidbeckham.com

INDEX

Page numbers for photographs are in **boldface** type.